Sexfunky

A collection of poetry, Volume IV

By Ayoka B.

AYOKA
Joyinhome Publishing

Sexfunky

Ayoka B.

Published by Joyinhome Publishing

ISBN: 979-8-9897325-5-5

Somewhere between love and lust... Sexfunky.

Sexfunky

Adoration is tattooed in your eyes

As you suck my big toe

And caress my velvety rose petals.

Broad shoulders to the narrow

Of your divine pelvis

The ink accentuating your caramel back.

Us,

We...

Sexfunky.

The tenderness you bestow on our children,

The magnetism of your natural swag,

The steady stroke of your brush

Awakens the butterflies like our first kiss.

Your skillful tongue travels

Across my collarbone

Down my spine

Up my thigh...

Tangled in our salty sheets

Us,

We...

Sexfunky.

The artistry of your hand

Brings color to a dismal world.

Your easy smile

Reminds me of lyrics we've shared

Through peaks and valleys, days and years

And the fire that burns white hot

Just beneath my skin.

I shiver at the thought.

Us,

We...

Sexfunky.

Gimme

Gimme...

Easy smiles

And food for my mind.

The gift my hips are hungry for.

Your heart in exchange for mine.

Time to truly know you

And urgent lips that melt into my fiery flesh.

Unlimited laughter and naughty thoughts

The opportunity for our souls to mesh.

Knowing hands

That find a new secret cove

Tenderness that I protect

With unending and crazy love.

I never thought of love as greedy,

Until now,

Until you.

Gimme.

When I sit on your throne,

I am home.

Your lovely dick

Fills me,

Igniting my nerves

As we climb upward.

It's this one thing that keeps me trippin'...

The thought of your hands

Caressing my body

Pushes my button

And I crave you.

My thighs clasp your face

As I rub my pussy

On your tongue,

Your lips,

Your mouth.

It's this one thing that keeps me trippin'...

I long to savor your taste

And lick your crown

Until my juices spill.

I am your strawberry love.

A Night Out

The percussion

Seems to move through me in slow motion.

The conga, the cowbell.

A dull ache ricocheted through the sinews

Of my body

And crevices of my thoughts.

Once again,

I could feel his touch-

Making slow, deliberate love.

The bass became my pulse

And the ache spread through my heart

Bringing a burn to my skin.

I was feverish

Remembering his gaze locked into mine.

The urgency

His mouth melting my flesh.

The heat of the music seduced me into a trance

And I felt his rhythm.

I swayed slowly

And with the crescendo of the drum

I transcended

My eyes wet

Limbs weak from the journey.

I felt exposed to the eyes watching me.

Tonight

I want to be free

To taste all of you.

Feel all of us- together.

To invite the shudders that you give to me only.

No wine, no music

Just our minds meeting.

Get lost with me.

In my eyes,

In my heart

In us.

Envy

Your intense gaze follows me.

The beautiful torture that is etched on your face

Excites me.

When your smoothness grazes my full lips,

She moistens and yearns to be filled.

The heat of your stare excites Her.

She becomes wet

Envious of my mouth.

Ode to Celibacy

The calendar is unkind
Charting the flight of time spent
Alone.

Absence as the norm
Is disconcerting.
Leading me to retrace the meandering path
That led to this
Desolate place.

I am a fiery Scorpion
Thrashing against the bars of
A self-imposed cage.

Although not without benefit...
That easily slips my mind
On quiet mornings
And silent nights.

Stutter

I watch you.

I see the moment

When you get lost,

Overcome with the high that you feel.

Sleepy eyes glaze over

And your mouth opens slightly

As if you are about to speak,

But no words come.

Your smile widens

And the dimples set in

As sweat rolls down your face,

And into my eyes

Talkin' shit

'Til your hip slips

And loses rhythm

Cuz the pussy made you stutter.

Too Much

Am I too much?

Sometimes, you want me to think I'm not enough,

But I'm enough when you're

Between these creamy thighs.

Too bossy?

Lay your ass down so I can sit on your face.

Too loud?

But you like it when I moan and scream your name,

Right?

Too moody?

Well right now, I'm in the mood for you to fuck me,

HARD.

Too direct?

I wanna suck the tip while you play with my pussy.

Too bitchy?

I am *that* bitch.

Too sexy?

I am a sexual being who won't apologize.

I'm a

Sexy

Moody

Strong,

Bitch

Who

May

Just

Be

Too

Much

For

YOU.

Kiss Me

Kiss me long and slow

To remind me that love is in your heart

Kiss me long and slow

And I know that I still ignite that spark.

Kiss me long and slow

So that my petals become soft and wet

Kiss me long and slow

And I'll make you cum so you'll never forget.

Kiss me long and slow

Because this pussy is yours alone

Kiss me long and slow

So my mouth can engulf my favorite bone.

Kiss me long and slow

While you fuck me and I moan

Kiss me long and slow,

Because your dick is my throne.

Ayoka B. explores the themes of Womanhood, identity, love, loss and family through poetry, fiction and nonfiction. Her writing is vulnerable and honest which resonates with readers. Through her unique lens as a Black woman and DC native, Ayoka seeks to share the untold stories of mothers, sisters, daughters, friends and wives. Her goal is to help people gain clarity and insight into their lives.

Ayoka has a professional background in public relations and strategic communications. She received a bachelor's degree in Communications from Temple University in Philadelphia, Pa. and a master's degree in Public Communication from American University in Washington, DC. Ayoka is a mother and lives with her family in Costa Rica.

This is the final poetry collection in a series of four books. Her debut novel, *Love At Second Sight*, published in 2024. Learn more at linktr.ee/joyinhome